MW01289294

LAND OF LOUD NOISES AND VACANT STARES:

POEMS OF WAR AND HEALING

PETER M. BOURRET

Land of Loud Noises and Vacant Stares: Poems of War and Healing

Copyright © 2015 Peter M. Bourret

Printed the USA by CreateSpace
Poetry / Nonfiction / Vietnam War / PTSD
First Edition (March, 2015)
First Printing (March, 2015)
ISBN-13: 978-1507715314
EAN-10: 1507715315

DEDICATION

This book of poetry is respectfully dedicated to the Marines and corpsmen of the First Battalion, Seventh Marine Regiment, First Marine Division, especially Dale Witzman of Charley Company, Mike Rae, a radio operator for 81mm mortars, Jim Shott, a friend from boot camp who also served on Hill 10, and Mike Brewer, my replacement in mortars and a fellow Tucsonan, and of course, the men in Bravo Section, 81mm mortars, and in particular, the men in my Jello Squad. In addition, these poems are especially dedicated to L.Cpl. Lawrence J. Vargas, a former member of my mortar squad, and Sgt. Thomas D. O'Connor, a great forward observer, both killed in 1968. Semper Fi.

CONTENTS

Acknowledgements
Preface

1 **Prologue:** the catechism of killing
  War's Puzzle Pieces
2 Existential Angst
3 war games
4 an existential flag
5 the *détente* dance
6 passing away Nam-style
7 twilight time: the sad version of the song
8 taking a hill
9 Alone with *it* on Veterans Day
10 steady employment in the Nam
11 Khe Sanh: the hill battles
12 when your number comes up
13 Khe Sanh: the siege
14 no rhyme or reason
15 listening to my inner Kubler-Ross
16 beatin' the back-in-the-world blues
17 words in the wind
18 the anatomy of dying under a February sky
19 the lesson plan plays out
20 *fng-words*
21 one of the cobblestones on the road to hell
22 the flying metal monster
23 I Fished that Pond
24 live-fire philosophy class
25 PTSD Blues
26 the Alice riddle
27 a poem for Pink Rat

28 of KIAs and WIAs
29 no good-night lullabies
30 Burial Detail
31 the glory of war
32 sorrow
33 what if I misspell a word
34 Hue City: February '68
35 Hemingways
36 I never met a gentle war
37 poor reception
38 gauntlet
39 shadow boxing
40 been on the road way too long
41 the corpses pile up
42 time and space in the rice paddies of yesterday
43 limping on the first leg of the journey home
44 sleeping through Memorial Day
45 seeing through the noise
46 twenty-four-hour hop-scotching
47 firing the bean counter and hiring the Buddhist
48 the word womb
49 pondering the possible geography of living
50 *mea culpa*
51 the comin' home two-step
52 the ambush merry-go-round
53 when coping falls short
54 casualty count ghosts
55 and maybe
56 fertilizer
57 the trigger guarantee
58 the alphabet of mail from the war zone
59 emancipation proclamation 1968
60 the art of healing

61 sunsets taste delicious
62 robert frost chats with hamlet about career moves
63 **Epilogue:** creative process
Index Of First Lines
About The Author
About The Artist

ACKNOWLEDGEMENTS

Although writing is a solitary venture, a number of people have helped me on this journey in a variety of ways. In addition to her support, Cheryl Watters was invaluable, helping me fine-tune my poems with her insightful observations. Numerous people have tirelessly encouraged and supported my writing efforts: my son Jeremy Bourret, Bob Kish, Megan Hughes, Sue & Chuck Peters, Liz & Michael Callahan, Carolyn Kittle, Chrystal Lynn, Forest Danford, Gretchen McFarron, Vicki & Howie Hibbs, Jeff Stensrude, Karen Schwabacher, Tina Carbo, Dave Barger, Dr. David Beil, Dr. Otto Kausch, Robin Mirante, Steve Johnson, Wendy LaFave, Dale Witzman, Ron Whiteman, Mike Fitz, Don Harmon, Jim Chard, Steven Bates, Pepper Pro, Michael (the work horse) & Lydia Brewer, Ryan Brewer, Phil Tully, John Lynch, Pat DeVito, Michaele Chapman, and Danetta Mecikalski, Rudy Saldivar, Erin Fitzgerald Jacobs, Rachel Milligan, Wendy Newell, Shirley Ward, and Hilary Quick--seven of my former students. Rose Pearson, the creative director and founder of The Writers' Circle, Inc., believed in me and published *WAR: a memoir* online. Mary Pat Sullivan, Damiana Cohen, Jerry Barkan, John Sole, Lynda Gibson, Marcus Conway, Barb Noel, Morris & Sharon Barkan, and Mary Bourret, my sister, have been a faithful audience, always willing to listen to my poetry and to offer feedback. I would be remiss if I failed to mention my mom, a gifted writer, tireless in her support of my love of writing. Bill Black has not only encouraged me and supported my writing but has been invaluable with his technical assistance, including the cover layout. I owe a thank-you to Jordan Danford for his help in making the cover come to fruition. I am also indebted to Denham Clements, a fellow Marine, who has supported my writing and has provided the artwork for the cover, which comes from his prize-winning piece "Vietnam Elegy." If I have forgotten someone, please forgive me. This won't be my last book, so I'll make sure I'll remember for the next one.

PREFACE

The puzzle pieces of war can vary greatly, but the connection becomes clear upon completion of the puzzle. The combatants stroll across the stage of the tragedy called war; unfortunately, they are only a portion of the cast of characters.

In my previous book of poetry, I address the concept of the physics of war: in the Nam, time and space followed their own set of rules. For many veterans, the vacant stares alluded to in my most recent book of war poetry mocked calendars and the Pacific Ocean, tunneling into their young hearts. Their bodies survived combat, but their souls have died. In the prologue, I address a key dilemma of war: coming home, which becomes very problematic and is a lifelong journey for many. War in the combat zone has a simplicity to it; one is either dead or alive, but post-war life at home gets complicated. Killing one's problems is no longer the best solution. On the long and circuitous journey home, many returning veterans often stumble and fall as they roam through a fog. Triggers abound and emotional ambushes lurk at every turn. The skills that brought about survival in the war zone tend to interfere with a *normal* life at home, so veterans often struggle to learn how to acclimate to life back in *the world*, which also impacts friends and family. The journey to healing is an arduous one for the friends and families of those killed in combat. The impact on mothers, fathers, brothers and sisters is profound and lasts a lifetime. A life full of opportunities is traded in for a flag folded in a triangle and a letter of thanks from "a grateful nation." Birthdays are remembered, but so are deathdays. Life is changed forever because death roams the battlefield, randomly picking who would live and who would die.

The reader will see the harsh realities of war; no sugarcoating to be found, and the euphemisms, so popular with politicians, will be absent. The reader will begin to understand the insidious terror felt by the young Marine who describes his reality when the sun escapes in the west and Charlie's on the move in the land of loud noises and vacant stares.

PROLOGUE

1. - the catechism of killing

war is deceptively simple
when the bullets are whizzing by
and shrapnel is racing for its finish line
war isn't complicated until you get home

WAR'S PUZZLE PIECES

2. - Existential Angst

Stars everywhere
Cricket chatter
Cold beads of sweat
meet my hand
as it roams the geography of my face
The thought is back:
someone in the darkness
wants to kill me

3. - war games

war is a four-letter word
but it's a delicious meal
for those who beat the drums and sound the bugles
always watching at a safe distance
directing traffic
and sending the true believers, the naive, the brave,
the bamboozled, and the fearful to the front:
to face the enemy
to send the evil adversaries to eternity
     to Allah and a martyr's afterlife orgy
     or maybe to the Sistine-Chapel-ceiling God
     or to a black hole of existential nothingness

mesmerized by war's magical music
the cadence of the drum beat
and the blare of the bugle
these sirens' sounds of the battle symphony
seduce these cavalier pretenders
supplicants bowing at the altar of Narcissus

but their nostrils have never known
the acrid smell of battle smoke
nor the seared-in-the-soul stench
of yesterday's rotting corpse
nor have they ever felt the ground tremble
from each rocket or artillery shell
that drops in to say hello
their ears have never heard the clatter of small-arms fire
nor the roar of a jet racing toward its target
and most certainly
the sounds of the wounded and the desperate dying
their screams, their moans, their final gasping
that sad sucking sound and the blood-red gurgling
none of this ever makes the long journey home
to the ears of these flag-draped politicians
obese in their panoply of patriotic platitudes
and while the smoke of battle still lingers
it's permanently Halloween
and the Helen Keller costume is their favorite

4. - an existential flag

an American flag sits on a shelf
waiting to drape a casket
waiting to honor a Marine
waiting to be handed to a mother

at the ambush site
Charlie waits patiently
then his bullets race across a rice paddy
and a Marine falls hard
his bullet-riddled body ready for the plane-ride home
to see his mom
his dead eyes staring into eternity

a stoic mother
will pull this flag to her bosom
a triangled thank-you from a grateful nation
that's what it will be called
but then tears will stream down her cheeks
as her little boy strolls across her memory
all this to be replaced:
a casket
a grave stone
a folded flag sits on a shelf

5. - the *détente* dance

last Tango with the Nam
a thought races through my head:
no more pushing me around

taking the lead on the dance floor
PTSD always runs the show
the alpha of the pack
the Fred Astaire of pain
leading
always leading me astray
commanding me to bow to my gnawing ache
I want to desert the dance floor
be AWOL in Margaritaville
but it's a forever dance with a twist:
musical chairs is now in session
I swap roles with my dance partner
taking the lead
spinning PTSD around
pulling it close
staring into its eyes
now weaker magnets
with each tear that slides down my cheeks

6. - passing away Nam-style

passing away Nam-style
precious time slipping away
tomorrow is obsolete
but there's no goodbye silence
no subtle sounds
as the last breath tiptoes to eternity
there's only a river of blood
this tapestry of death painted angry red
this burial shroud woven with terrible threads
no euphemisms to be found
been shot between the eyes
but the screaming
  the begging
  the gasping
are the notes in the soundtrack
that slices through decorum
through the burning May heat
through teenage flesh
  wishing for love
  wishing for tomorrow
  wishing for a beer
  wishing for anything else
but Charlie plays a different game
and you're the bull's-eye
no matter how much you promise God anything
but God's on a cloud
and you're on a stretcher
and you wish the corpsman had magic
but all he has is morphine
  and sadness buried deep in his eyes

but does this narrative matter
when breathing belongs to others
when dreams belong to others
when tomorrow belongs to others
and you wish you were your grandfather
seventy-four
with family
with the luxury
of passing away

7. - twilight time: the sad version of the song

in the world of the war zone
it's always twilight
that time just before the sun sets
for some sorry soul
soon to have a bullet blast through his head
or bits of shrapnel in his heart
the setting sun says its goodbyes
to the boys soon to be dead
on jungle trails or by rice paddy dikes
the yawning sun doesn't care
about these characters in the dead-end story--
where they see their final sunset
it just slips away in the west as usual
while drained and empty-eyes stare into the mud
or peer skyward toward invisible clouds

twilight time evaporates quickly for the dead
but not for the grunts
still humping through the jungle
or slogging through a rice paddy
the sun will set for some
bullets or shrapnel will be their tickets
but for the fortunate who fly home
twilight time will always linger
over staying its welcome
but no menacing metal
flying through the twilight air

but for some the sun will set in their hearts
that will never know the pastel ribbons
of the morning tapestry
the sunrise
a town crier
announcing a new day

8. - taking a hill

corpses strewn randomly across the ridgeline
their dead eyes staring into the spring fog
jets strafing the boys from Up North
soon to be buried in their bunkers on 861
an instant cemetery
and the first hill to fall
but this victory for the boys from the heartland
is just a down payment for 881 north and south
hills shrouded in mist and battle smoke
soon to fade away
and when victory and defeat are tasted
always bitter
always pungent
the medals won won't matter
as much as the memories of Marines
staying with their dead
protecting their wounded
those granite images
lurking in the land of nightmares
and soaking in blood
some morbid memories matter
some are draped with pride

9. - Alone with *it* on Veterans Day

it makes you feel good
to parrot patriotic phrases
that flow out of one side of your mouth
you thank the troops
but you don't see the thousand-yard stare
in their vacant teenage-eyes
nor do you see the tears that flow
from those sometimes silent eyes
and admonitions roll out of the other side of your mouth
reminding me to not be so angry
and to *just get over it*
but my dream landscape is laden with land mines
and my road is fraught with ancient booby traps
and ambushes lurk at every turn
even when the sun blesses me with a soothing smile
and yes, I want to believe in magic again
but *it* is more than monosyllabic
more than a convenient and casual pronoun
it was an all-expenses-paid trip
to Dante's seventh circle of hell
where I was keelhauled
through a river of boiling blood and fire
better known on your map as Vietnam
and I've read *The Myth of Sisyphus*
and shared a few beers with Hamlet
the smartest dumb prince in the land
and he's my hero
because he isn't one

and I guess I'm still married to my tragic flaw
with no divorce in sight
because there always seems to be an ambush
waiting patiently
to send its shrapnel to my heart
but never able to kill it
because when I bleed
there's no blood
only coming-home tears

the National Anthem makes you cheer
when you hear it at a basketball game
but when the words about *the rockets' red glare*
explode in my ears
my Medicare heart is twenty again as the ground shakes
and the crowd melts away
and in the black night
a ball of fire and a deafening forever noise
sets my heart racing
I've got those jackhammer-blues,
so I beg my Catholic God
to light the candles on my twenty-first birthday cake
and make them stop their rockets
from trying to send me home early
but then a volley of three more rockets crash into our hill
and I want to jump on the first chopper out of town
with a direct flight to section seventeen,
row twenty-seven,
seat five,
McKale Center,
Tucson,
Arizona,
USA

where the National Anthem
is nothing more than feel-good words
the starting gun for a basketball game
but these star-spangled words overrun my heart
this time
every time
and I feel each letter in *the rockets' red glare*
just words for the fortunate fans
who only hear those feel-good lyrics
but the letters in these words
are like tenacious shards of shrapnel
and I'm the magnet
Oh, say, can you see, by the dawn's early light?
and the tears welling up in my eyes
always answering *yes*

10. - steady employment in the Nam

patiently lurking
playing the long game
death has many gears

it carries a to-do list
constantly crossing out this name, then that
death has honed its skills
homing in with a primal radar
racing through the air
hungry for a home
it hovers patiently
or sometimes stalks in silence
but always waits for the perfect moment
to pounce on the prey

11. - Khe Sanh: the hill battles

when the math of mayhem is in session
more than a thousand mothers will weep
wondering why so many sons must die
and they'll casually be called the casualty count
these boys from Up North
and these boys from across the sea
none of it will add up
because subtraction is this week's lesson
and a minus sign will always make a mother hate math

12. - when your number comes up

no passport required,
so the big guns roll out of caves
hurling their death language
across a border
to a hill with a number
861
the area code for death
861
another page in Marine Corps history
861
the last page in too many memoirs
861
a pin on a map
861
a victory for someone
861
a hill in Hell
861
the station for the sweet chariot ride home
861
a place to survive
861
but
when your number is up
surviving 861 isn't enough
because
Agent Orange falls effortlessly
floating like a million invisible leaves
through the afternoon sky
like slow-motion shrapnel
taking its sweet time

no quick kill
slow death wrapping its hands around the throat
of the survivor
one of the fortunate few
shrapnel from the Nam doesn't care how it kills you
in an instant
roaring in from a cave
or
slowly and silently
tip-toeing through decades
finally hitting its mark
killing with cancer
where shrapnel failed to cut young flesh
death is patient
as the casualty count keeps climbing

13. - Khe Sanh: the siege

fourth of July fireworks come early
for those hunkered down in a hole
home is where the mud is
home is where the shrapnel isn't

14. - no rhyme or reason

the language and the landscape of my poetry
may lacerate your sensibilities
and rhyming never knocks on my door,
so please help me find the rhyming match
for the words in the lexicon that I carry in my heart
death
shrapnel
blood
explosion
funeral
purple heart
KIA

why would rhyming words
hang out in a neighborhood called the Nam?

15. - listening to my inner Kubler-Ross

now I gotta move yesterday's grief
to the front of the line
back in the day I had no time to sob
no time to say goodbye
too busy stayin' alive
droppin' a bead on Charlie
sendin' him to visit his ancestors

16. - beatin' the back-in-the-world blues

dance with your distractions
or dance with your demons
pulling the boogeyman close
smell its pungent breath
penetrating the power
peering into the eyes of feelings feared
and you'll find a deceptive devil,
so dance away the fear of feeling
letting the tears slide slowly down your cheeks
as the demon walks away
defeated by the stern and gentle gaze in your eyes
the gateway to your soul
on this emancipation day
when you decide to finally come home
trembling and stumbling

17. - words in the wind

War and Peace, Hamlet,
The Adventures of Huckleberry Finn
each hungry for a bookcase or a library shelf
instead discarded and lying on the ground
the pages flapping in the breeze

Tolstoy clutching a half-empty bottle of vodka
and wearing a Russian question mark
and Shakespeare's goateed head
shaking back and forth
like an obedient metronome
obeying the perfect rhythm of iambic pentameter
and morose Mark Twain's tears flooding the Mississippi
while thousands of words
some in clusters
some as single silent words
float away
and behind them
Death,
loitering and sporting a smirk,
watches as the pages fan in the wind
and more words and phrases,
all more beautiful than the vibrant ribbons of color
in an Arizona sunset
and metaphors sent by the muse,
all meant to be tasted
and entire paragraphs of prose,
all gifts from the word factory
on the other side of the universe
and stanzas of poetry,
all stolen from the gods

it all floats away in the hot afternoon air
and somewhere in the heartland
a mother sheds those terrible tears
that only a mother can know
because perfectly placed pieces of shrapnel
racing through the hot afternoon air
in a place called the Nam
always trump an almost masterpiece
or even a dime-store novel
and the blank, white pages of the novel that never was
flap in the wind

18. - the anatomy of dying under a February sky

the killing bullet
or piece of shrapnel
just shows up unannounced
that's the rule
dripping with bad manners
rarely knocking
all business
nothing personal of course
just working like any other Joe
if it could wax philosophical
it might say
you were never meant to be more than eighteen
I didn't write your script
and one more casualty
or a son
or a friend
or a father
or a husband
or a brother
one more body will bleed out
under a February sky
painted with the bleakest shade of gray
a callous confederate color
one more time

19. - the lesson plan plays out

boot camp isn't a philosophy class
the killing curriculum is blunt:
kill VC kill
left right left
ah, the rhythm of cadence
how poetic
the themes are simple
nothing erudite
stand and fight
make Charlie die for his country
kill VC kill
left right left
and the price of your soul
a dress blue uniform
that'll get you laid
and
down the road
your jungle utilities can get you killed
left right left
one foot in front of the other
Charlie is comin'
left right left
GI numba ten
kill GI kill
and when the morning sneaks away
to wherever mornings go
one will still be standing
left right left
kill kill kill

20. - *fng-words*

there's the *f-word*
a favorite of drill instructors and twelve-year-old rebels
there's the *n-word*
a favorite of rappers and whiter than snow racists
and then
there are the terrible twins
the *g-words*
that haunt combat vets
guilt
a rusty bayonet to the heart
and
grief
a sentence of sadness and sorrow
both terrible twins torturing the soul
until
the monsoon season begins

21. - one of the cobblestones on the road to hell

snuggling up to violence as a means of fighting violence
French kissing the viper's venom is tricky
a seductive solution
but be careful
of seeing wisdom in dancing with a rattlesnake
because when I kill my evil enemy
I stab a dagger into my heart
and the Buddha never rejoices in a soul's suicide
neatly wrapped up in good intentions
when I fire at the evil doer
and my bullet passes through his heart
and thanks to the Buddhist Laws of Physics
the bullet boomerangs
doing a world tour
returning home to my heart
and ricocheting endlessly in the deep caverns of my soul
because the physics of violence
is like a letter mailed with the wrong address
return to sender

22. - the flying metal monster

in the world of war
metal maims
and in the mayhem
plowshares are mocked
just useless machines

shrapnel roams the battlefield endlessly
like a shark
a hungry hunter prowling
ready to burrow its razor sharp teeth into young flesh
and into the hearts of families far away
but only tasting the delicious dying blood
of boys with useless to-do lists
but never tasting the anguish
nor the sorrow sown in the hearts
of mothers who bore their boys
not so long ago

23. - I Fished that Pond

Didn't feel like waking up dead.
Meandering through the rice paddies,
death is hungry for its next meal.
The menu, endless in its choices.

Strolling casually through the rice paddies,
death smiles
as it plays the eeny-meeny-miny-mo game,
its whimsical finger
finally settling on a grunt.

Nothing personal.
The grunt is picked for the one team
only suicides want to be on.
He just wanted
to not be the last one picked
back on the playground
back when he was a kid
with sad eyes.
The metronome of fate,
like wiper blades,
rhythmical and nonchalant,
now yawning
and no longer interested
in the grunt's dead and vacant eyes,
staring up
into someone else's blue sky

24. - live-fire philosophy class

mortality on steroids
our foolish notions about being invincible
our youthful hubris
so certain about our immortality
teenage Greek gods packin' M16s
callin' in air strikes and mortars on Charlie
while our girlfriends dance the night away
at the senior prom

in the Nam
shrapnel and bullets were for some other unlucky soul
but the Nam slapped us down
putting us in our place
like a Jesuit professor of logic
unmercifully
squeezing every bit of intellectual arrogance
out of an answer-ridden student
such a bright boy but such sloppy thinking
look all around
toss away your delusional glasses
those are body bags over there
and KIA isn't a car
KIA is what they call you
when breathing and birthdays
and girlfriends and tomorrow's plans
belong to others

25. - PTSD Blues

I've got those PTSD blues
they make me crazy
and crave the booze
to help the past be hazy

been on the road way too long
stumbling and falling down
wonderin' what went wrong
and why I wear this frown

I ache to finally come home
from this endless journey
but seems I just roam
and search to be free

oh, I've got those PTSD blues
they make me crazy
but coming home is what I choose
the choice is clear not hazy

oh, I've got those PTSD blues
but coming home is what I choose

26. - the Alice riddle

in the binary black and white world of the Nam
red was an honorary color on the pallet
replacing gray
an inconvenient war-zone color
always hanging around and causing trouble
too many strings attached to guilt
nothing more than a hangman's noose
and all those ethical pop quizzes
and the anguish of existential angst,
so
who has time for a catechism
when *thou shalt not kill*
hangs out with an asterisk
and Alice won't even venture out of the rabbit hole
because
in the Nam
they shoot anything
in a free-fire zone
including Lewis Carroll characters
and Alice knows
that if you're dead
you're a Viet Cong
but she never hung out with Ho Chi Minh
she was too busy doing the existential dance
with the Cheshire Cat
and being ambushed by the Mad Hatter's riddles

but there's one thing for certain,
Alice already knows the answer
to the free-fire zone riddle
how many bullets does it take to riddle a body?

instead, the Mad Hatter asks:
how long does it take to get your soul back?
and Alice replies:
I didn't know I had lost it
and the Mad Hatter says:
then stay in the rabbit hole
so you don't get your head blown off
since it wouldn't be good
for either body or soul

27. - a poem for Pink Rat

young love
the stuff of sappy songs
you owned a monopoly on that
we laughed at you
for being so whipped
your stacks of love letters
perfect proof
but we secretly wished
for those letters written from the heart
but all we got were Dear Johns,
C-rations,
one more day to cross off on our tours of duty,
and the people in the darkness
        full of deadly intention and little love

we were their goal
the dead and going home version
but who wants to think about that

so
we laughed
mocking our friend
never telling him
that our teenage-hearts burned with jealousy

28. - of KIAs and WIAs

the circuitous route of the random battle bullet
blasting the bull's-eye
never missing its mark
with the squeeze of the trigger
the damage done
the soul
dripping off the trigger finger of the shooter
foolishly believing his eyes
that he's killed his enemy
but this was only
the first firefight of soul suicide

29. - no good-night lullabies

oh, to slumber
to surrender to somatic silence
as a full citizen of the dream world
the land hidden deep
behind eyelids drawn like a window shade
where it's safe to play a role in a nightmare
as the main attraction in the nocturnal theater
oh, to be a player in a nightmare during sleep time
startled and then awakening
being held closely by a mother
as she wipes away the sweat
from a four-year-old's forehead
but mom never made it to the Nam,
so I settle for shallow sleep
safe and just below the surface
where no nightmare fantasies
have time to roam in the sleep world
and under the jet black blanket called night
my real nightmares lurk
demon armies
waiting patiently
their hearts pounding
to the restless rhythm of the death drum
and the killing cadence
soon to be the soundtrack
of an ambush

mom is still nowhere to be found,
so I seek solace
snuggling up to my M16
stoic trepidation surges through my veins
this scenario is chiseled into my granite soul
buried deep in the black hole of malevolent memory
always lingering
as I hunger
for the beaming smile of the early morning sun

30. - Burial Detail

There were too many dead to bury,
so
I buried my
anger
fear
guilt
and
loneliness
in the red clay
of a place we called the Nam
Who's got time to grieve
when
Charlie's comin' to send me home early

31. - the glory of war

in war
there's no tragic hero strolling across the stage
the only characters
> the victor
>> a delusional fool believing the lie
> the vanquished
>> those rotting in defeat believing nothing

participants in folly
> the victor and the vanquished
>> but never a winner
>> only losers

32. - sorrow

the soul saturated in ancient anguish
drowns in the river of sorrow
meandering like the Mississippi
running deeper than the currents of the River Styx
but always searching for the ocean

33. - what if I misspell a word

the teacher's red pen was a deadly dagger
killing the desire to write
misspelled words flowed like a river
and the boogeyman's crossed arms bellow disapproval
he's waiting to pounce on my paper with his pen,
so writing about my PTSD will just be an ambush
I will spell trauma with two *M*s
> pain with an *E*
> guilt without a *U*
> and fear with two *E*s
spelling is a crap shoot
and fear found its way into my heart
long before Charlie started shooting at me

34. - Hue City: February '68

like tenement cockroaches swarming
when the light's switched on
Charlie is everywhere
hungry for blood
ready to beat Dracula at his game
the Perfume River stinks of death
and the reporter adds it all up:
one and one are zero
February aha moments
explode in Walter Cronkite's brain
and when the battle is done
although dead Charlie is everywhere
the three-letter president
has had enough
looking to Texas
and a social security check
but back in Hue
another page in Marine Corps history
still waits for the blood-red ink to dry

35. - Hemingways

if you don't want to hear about war
don't send the young to it
quite simply
some will come home
all will be changed forever
some will sit in silence
some will write about it
their ticket on the plane home
once upon a time
a Marine wanted to be a man

36. - I never met a gentle war

you crave gentle words that sing you to sleep
those soothing sounds of a patriot's lullaby
but the madness I parade in front of you
has an uncomfortable marching cadence
and a rhyme scheme that's been shot dead

my words ambush your fairytale
void of anguished images
all as sharp
all as cutting
all as burning
as the random bits of shrapnel
that exploded their way through teenage flesh
into the sinews of the soul
now with forever scars
forever memories
and a purple heart
and salt and pepper hair
if you were lucky

37. - poor reception

like an Old Testament prophet
I roam the desert
my circuitous road home
through sand storms
and cold black nights

and when I tell my story
my grief is wrapped in grating words
too gritty for the deaf
who read my lips
and wish they were blind
and who run from my words
sharp razor blades
slicing through their marshmallow movie
slashing to the truth
to the blood-red reality
the cold and cruel clarity
the carnage that is war
where even a flag unfurled fails
to soak up the blood of boys
who believed in their cause
just long enough to get shot dead

so when I speak these words
that well up from my yesterdays
the deaf always scurry away to bow to their idol
the monkey with its hands
cupped over its ears
but I wait patiently

38. - gauntlet

dipped in vinegar
with no sugary sweetness to soothe
no patriotic phrases oozing from my mouth
my poetry is unsettling for you
my in-your-face words are inconvenient,
so you squirm
drowning in disgust
as you long for the lazy lie about heroism
and your righteous tongue
painted red white and blue
mumbles your dissatisfaction

my story is a sandwich
but there's no flag unfurled and wrapped around it
just a question mark standing tall
in this single-sentence story
lasting forty-five years too long
a run-on sentence from hell
sprinkled with war's words
all neighbors in the dictionary of destruction:
death
anger
pain
sorrow
shrapnel
shame
dying
killing
guilt
grief

but there are better bookends also:
courage and camaraderie

a trio of American colors finds a home in my narrative
but they're a different shade from the patriotic paint
the sacred trinity of colors
that decorates the portrait in your star-spangled fantasy

with deadly intention and painting in earnest
death dipped its brush in the perfect paint for the occasion
dabbing with delight
a blood-red punctuation mark
a bullet hole in a Marine's head
and then another in his chest
the afternoon was still young
and the Angel of Death would return another day

killing 101 was a pass-fail course
combat was not art class
no paint-by-numbers
no staying within the lines
just portraits painted with pain
to be hung in the hearts of mothers
yet for the Marine with the shot-dead dreams
just a landscape laced with metaphors:
  a final sky--
  his new home with a fresh coat of blue paint,
  a long and lazy cloud--
  his white burial shroud,
  a dusty dead-end road--
  his ink blotter drenched in red
  the final punctuation mark in his simple sentence

meanwhile in the land-of-the-free
some people jibber-jabber in patriotic tongues
with empty words and hearts that are wastelands
with no bumper crop of compassion in sight
these blind people never see Kubler-Ross
hiding in a bunker
nor the Grim Reaper
strolling through a rice paddy
or under a jungle canopy
or on a dusty-red-clay road to nowhere
for a Marine who lost the fifteenth round with a bullet
and bled a red that belongs only to the dead
leaving each letter in his name to soak away
he will never get the chance
to write his story
but rest assured
someone who wouldn't like the way it sounds
won't be able to spit in his face someday

so ladies and gentlemen,
patriots all,
you can keep your parades
it just would be nice
if you had some manners
and didn't mutter about the story I tell
but you did
spitting your mumbled words in my face like it was 1968
but you're not a protestor
you're a patriot,
so this scenario burns more painfully
than mortar shrapnel cutting to the bone

I also used to believe in fairytales
but the Nam is a free-fire zone
where even the Easter Bunny wouldn't be safe
thank you, ma'am
for reminding me
that bad manners are nothing new
been goin' on from way back when
making it possible for a nailed-up Jesus to say:
Father forgive them,
for they know not what they do

so I guess I'll listen to these words
and thank the lady
who spit her disrespectful words my way
'cause I can practice forgiveness
the currency that will pay my toll on the road home

but these wise words of forgiveness
        so delicious to my mind
still need to meander
and find their way to my heart
and the rich soil awaiting a healing harvest

39. - shadow boxing

shadow over there
a portrait in black
and I'm stumbling on a road
leading east
leading west
leading north
leading south
leading nowhere
my shadow is my partner
on this lonely highway home
but in my nightmare story
I'm only pretending
blind to the terrible truth
I'm the shadow
an obedient slave
subservient
as my master moves me to and fro on a whim
I'm the shadow
of loneliness
of anxiety
of anger
of guilt
of fear
when will I lead the dance
and not be the slave
but be myself again
just be me
just be?

40. - been on the road way too long

the flag unfurled
the sound of bagpipes
the cadence of the drum beat
the blare of the bugle
sights unseen
sounds never heard

your parade would be a little late
the time machine is in the shop
and sci-fi is just Santa Claus in outer space
and I stopped being six way back when,
so forget the should-have-been mantra
and the martini mixed with guilt
scrape the wax out of your ears
let your listening
be my welcome home parade
I'm easy to please
keep your medals
and open up your ears
the on-ramp to your heart
because
my words about war aren't stories
some Homeric sagas
to set your patriotic heart pounding
nor are they horror stories
on a channel you want to change
they are just my footsteps
on my road home

41. - the corpses pile up

twenty is the limbo year
a holding pattern between adolescence and adulthood
a time to ponder tomorrow's plans
imagining the possibilities of dreams yet to come
but war has a way of wiping innocence away
twenty is a time to kill
to be or not to be
that is my question
not Hamlet's
I answer with death language
and for the fortunate few
my mortar rounds maim
but my diary holds my killing proof
the numbers adding up
  each day
  each week
  each month
  each enemy dead
nameless characters in my killing story
if they're lucky
they're buried in a shallow grave
their friends saying their goodbyes
but that usually's not the case
war goes by its own set of rules
no time for formal funerals

I bury the numbers
proof of my killing skill
but time betrays me
it doesn't heal all wounds
my diary sits in a box in a closet
and the memory of that killing year
slowly percolates to the surface of my *now*
no matter what I do

now a twenty-year-old wearing white hair
wonders why tears roll down his cheeks
after so long
the aha moment is a mallet smashed against his heart
as he realizes he was a serial killer through and through
his death math adding up
when he asks for forgiveness
the priest will tell him
they were communists
your job was to kill them
but he remembers Catholic catechism class
when he knew the right answers
it was so simple then
but in the Nam
thou shalt not kill had an asterisk by it
but he wonders what Jesus would say
then he buries his questions
buries his tears
until the ambush shows up as it always does
a torrent of tears always tells the true story
killing was my calling card

42. - time and space in the rice paddies of yesterday

the half-life of a well-placed AK-47 round
    isn't only counted in years

like a perfectly rolled bowling ball hitting one pin
    then knocking over all the pins around it
    war's wounds of the heart
        wind their way through warriors
        wondering why
        waiting for answers
            playing hide-and-seek
            better than Charlie ever did

43. - limping on the first leg of the journey home

the killing country called the Nam
a catalyst catapulting me toward a fresh set of eyes
but first
drowning me in pain
thrusting a bayonet deep into my soul
twisting it
slicing the throat of my youth
enjoying it
so matter-of-factly
laughing
nothing personal

blind to the lessons looming
I stumbled and fell
prisoner to my delusions
that everything was alright
until that midnight hour
when the demons of yesterday
escape the land of the lie
scurrying from the subterranean world of fear and guilt
where the foolish wallow in the folly of deceit
believing that coming home is about an airplane trip
back to America
and completely unaware
that
like the Hotel California
no one gets out alive

44. - sleeping through Memorial Day

a laid-back holiday
with the early retirement plan
that people run from
your own personal holiday
stenciled in stone
oh, to be guzzling down a bottle of beer
and eating one too many hot dogs
but that's not the case
for the guest of honor

45. - seeing through the noise

my silence screams at me
the cicada symphony boldly blaring
this auditory irony
nothing more than a theme for Simon and Garfunkel
the one o'clock sun
compassionate Buddha eye in the western sky
smiles warmly
the noisy silence *is*
the duck gliding effortlessly through the water *is*
the one-o'clock sky masquerading as blue wallpaper *is*
and I *am*
one thread in this tapestry
of sound
of sight
of warmth
as my smile flows through the screaming army of cicadas

46. - twenty-four-hour hop-scotching

tinnitus is no Roman general
but just one more gift from the Nam
drowning my ears
with the not-so-subtle sound
of an ocean of cicadas roaring
a cacophony murdering the silence
no meditative moments
no escape from this tsunami of sound
and its deafening din
until I start my shift in the dream factory
where nightmares relentlessly roll off the assembly line
I ache for outsourcing
or a business bankruptcy
and when I open my eyes
stepping off the nocturnal elevator
the aroma of coffee kisses me
but yesterday's demons are itching to say hello
they love the smell of java
and they've got my address

then a knock on my door arrives without a hint
nothing preemptive
as with any good ambush
Emily Post doesn't tag along
been shot in the head and very dead,
so only the startling banging
the unwanted pounding
the hello from the hounds of hell
sending the calendar pages flipping backward
as I fasten my seat belt
on the speed-of-light express

but when it slams on the brakes
my twenty-year-old face flies through the windshield
there is no blood
only tears hungry to escape
and a heart pounding
echoing yesterday's killing cadence

pain's clock lives in the Jungian time zone
where satchel charges
thrown silently into the night air
explode with angry intention
and body parts
blown through the black nightmare
are just glad the trip to the ground is a short one

screaming cicadas serenade me
and slumped and sitting on the couch
I wipe away another round of tears
I only know of two places where cicadas fear to tread:
in dreamland,
where hungry wolves roam restlessly,
howling nightmare lyrics
and
in Shakespeare's undiscovered country,
where calendar pages flap forever,
finding no time for rest

so I smile as I unwrap my gift
a lifetime of noisy silence
because yesterday's bullets and shrapnel ignored me
they were busy sending other passengers to KIA country
where they will never hear the noisy silence
nor see another sunset sneaking away in the west

47. - firing the bean counter and hiring the Buddhist

my tears are older than my children
I am a grandfather
and somewhere in the universe
there is a ledger with a number
one I ache to know
the number of unshed tears
one or a million and counting
someday
the debt will be paid
and the best number in the world
will be zero

the smiling Buddha opens the elevator door
inviting in the cool afternoon air
for a slow ride to the ground floor
and my diaphragm is smiling

zero is only a number
and life isn't a math class
watches and calendars are charlatans
just tricks
keeping me hooked on my temporal heroin
called yesterday and tomorrow
but in my head I know it's a lie
that's kept me strung out on the illusion
that the past and the future exist

but my unsubtle anguish
from a thousand yesterdays ago
was born in the womb called my heart
so
I inhale the fresh aroma of this singular moment
and the blue skies above me
tip-toe through the canyons of my lungs
caressing and kissing me
with the *now* of the present moment
and for this instant
the ledger with the secret number of my unshed tears
floats away
I feel the breath
and not yesterday's pain
the rhythm of my breath
caresses a child's heart
hungry for a mother's gentle hug
as I breathe in God's penicillin

48. - the word womb

words
sometimes wicked and seductive
enticing me to march in place
to linger in a bunker
on a patrol
in a firefight
all reruns in my head

words
sometimes wondrous
healing
drawing me closer to home
to say hello to goodbye
to laugh again
to feel completely
to forgive

words
their birth place
their playground
the heart
that healing place
but words that roam
the dark and dangerous
back alleys of the mind
are anchors to yesterday

and the ship will never sail across the ocean
to a new land
where memories
are nothing more than scars healed

words
from the heart
draw me closer
to the distant shore
to that place I call home

49. - pondering the possible geography of living

how will my life's landscape lie
once I cut that final stand of barbed wire
and dismantled the final sandbag
that have encased my heart?

50. - *mea culpa*

the script
    fire mission
    ten H.E. rounds
    three confirmed kills
    excellent coverage of target
over time this template takes its toll,
so I bury the numbers
but not deep enough
just doin' my job
    a mantra so logical
but in the Nam
the math of guilt
adds up slowly:
    no pencil-and-paper-school-day exercise
    ink and a tattoo needle and my Catholic heart
    pumping guilt like West Texas oil

    no shiny gold star on my math homework
    because all my problems added up
    the sacred correct answer
    was nowhere to be found in the Nam

the target always had a mother and a father
war-zone math gets complicated
for altar boys who graduated from counting Hail Marys
to counting the enemy casualties
advanced math,
Nam-style

51. - the comin' home two-step

trolling for a dance partner
intrigued, I flirted with guilt,
the narcissist's friend,
but in the end,
it's a nowhere adventure
one to be chased by others

and guilt,
a lazy charlatan wearing the mask of responsibility,
became nothing more
than a homely freshman girl,
the one sporting a flat chest,
the one waiting for Godot
to ask her to dance

oh, to dance the night away--
so I wore the mask of Fred Astaire
but when the music stopped
shame was my dance partner
and this one-night stand
rolled through countless calendars
wreaking havoc like a German Panzer division
having Poland for lunch
and the stench of this demon lingered
no matter how much cologne I would splash on
until I shed the vampire's fear finally
and peered into the mirror
now watching Fred Astaire tip his hat
as he strolls away
and the putrid smell of shame
hitches a ride on the next cloud out of town

and I stand naked
relishing my wrinkles,
just mile posts on my long road home

52. - the ambush merry-go-round

the Animals' "Sky Pilot"
with its soul-catching sounds of bagpipes
and lyrics laced with ten thousand daggers
racing to my heart
is just one more classic song from the '60s
for the casual listener
but on this Sunday night
yesterday is a million miles away
yet magically camping next door
this antiwar anthem
nothing more than the remote control
played with by the karma god
knowing something that's over the horizon for me,
and so there's a click
on that surreal channel changer
sending me back to the well
to fetch another bucket of tears
one more time
as a tingling sensation rushes over me
overrun by the adrenaline army
I surrender to battalions of memories
crystal clear and made too real
my prayer at the altar where abracadabra is king
oh, please,
let these be mile posts on my road home
then the Animals are done
but the fat lady hasn't sung
and I know that tomorrow looms with ambushes
but in my gray-haired world
the shrapnel is parked in yesterday's garage
I'm safe

and I know I will never drown from my tears
a man living in the desert
always appreciating water

53. - when coping falls short

you cover your pain with a cynical mask
still wearing the war paint
everyday is Halloween
but no mask
no casual costume
can hide the pain painted across your face
    punctuated by stories buried
        deep in your eighteen-year-old heart
        hopelessly hiding in your wounded soul

a tired and wrinkled brow,
a signpost of time for some
but not for you
the furrows of your frown
cut deep like rivulets of regret
as a thousand *whys* parade in front of you
and your bad-mannered pain screams
through silent aching eyes
glued to yesterday's nightmares
reruns on the death channel
where's a commercial when you need one?

54. - casualty count ghosts

I guess the dead
did their time in Purgatory
or maybe they got a weekend pass
not sure
but they reminded me the other night
that I buried their dreams in an early grave
unfortunately my magic wand doesn't work
and I don't know the Lazarus trick,
so yesterday's dead stay dead
they haunt my heart that hopes for healing
but then I remember Lady Macbeth
with indelible red on her hands
and I hope Shakespeare's story
belongs solely to a Scottish lady
with murder on her mind
and I wonder how the Bard would write my story
as I ponder my tragic flaw
one more time
on the road home

55. - and maybe

I don't know where you are
or if you even exist
but I need to meet you
I ache to tell you my story
awash in tears
of that time when I padlocked my heart
double-sand bagged it
shot feelings on sight
but I was a younger man then
and the death of innocence
was as fresh as the aroma of grandma's apple pie
but the Nam has no time for this foolishness
the Nam only has time for fear and death
but I long for the day
when I find
one woman who will listen
to the feelings hiding behind the story of my Nam
she is there
maybe
willing to let the Nam roam through her ears
through her soul
and maybe
she'll peer into my eyes
and say *I love you*
with arms that hold me
and maybe
someday
there will be this corpsman-up moment
maybe

56. - fertilizer

partners of water bo dung
          nineteen-year-old
                    heroes' bodies—
                              white
                              yellow
                              black
                              brown
          school boys
                    turned warriors
                              drained
                                        lifeless
          subject
                    of
                              the
                                        telegram
son...fertilized...rice...paddies...
with...valor...and...honor...thanks...
lady...PS...your...son...and...medal...
to...follow...
STOP

57. - the trigger guarantee

all triggers aren't found on guns
some are replete with bad manners
forgetting to ask permission to drop in
they just show up
in your back yard
or as you're driving down the road
the where and the when
always tattooed with question marks
but triggers come with a lifetime guarantee
they'll appear at the most inopportune time
not their concern

58. - the alphabet of mail from the war zone

he sent a dead letter home
and of course they were shocked
when the official visit beat it
to their door step
and offered his mom and dad
three letters from the Nam
KIA

59. - emancipation proclamation 1968

integration of the races
        worked
        today
    applause
        a white boy
        a black boy
        a brown boy
        a yellow boy
   ALL
        got together

EQUALITY TODAY
        the boys
   ALL
        lay in the paddies
           drained
           of
           their
           red
           blood...
free   at   last

60. - the art of healing

for years I've painted the story of the Nam with words
now I dip a paint brush in my patient tears
waiting for permission
to roll down the canvas of my face
a landscape lost in time

61. - sunsets taste delicious

as I write this poem
I fade away
imaging:
a bullet whizzing by my nose
take-two:
I'm three inches closer than back then
the physics of a bullet finds my face
and I prove Newton right
dead weigh dropping to the ground
my dreams evaporating
like air in a busted balloon
these lines of poetry disappearing
like scenes in a dream
quickly forgotten before morning coffee

my two sons
my granddaughter
all my poems
all the chapters in my life
summed up succinctly
but not so neatly for my family nor my friends

Lance Corporal Peter M. Bourret, USMC
Killed In Action
Vietnam
June 7, 1968

but fate directed the movie
with no death scene
with no eulogy
with no casket

so the alphabet didn't shrink to three letters
KIA
and the number system
stretched past twenty
and computer keys pound
and sunsets await
because fate follows the script

62. - robert frost chats with hamlet about career moves

you babble your euphemisms
like they're the truth
for you
war was inconvenient

let's get a few things straight:
I didn't make war
while
you made love

I killed people
while I was exhausted
you fucked girls
while you were stoned

I learned the trigonometry of death
dropping mortar rounds
on the boys from Up North
you learned the math of marijuana
dropping a ten spot
for a bag of sweet Mary Jane

I yelled *incoming!*
you screamed *hell no, we won't go!*

I couldn't have spotted the Viet Cong in a line up
you couldn't have spotted Cupid on Valentine's Day

I used my skills to kill
hated the lifers
felt death's cold stare
you used girls for your pleasure
hated the GIs
felt groovy about the whole thing

I tripped out on the adrenaline rush
of tracer rounds slicing up the black night
you tripped out on the psychedelic rush
of LSD expanding your mind

I just knew that I was alive
until I was dead
you knew all the answers
because you lived in your head

now your hair is gray
and you joke that you have no memories of the Sixties
because you were stoned
everyone laughs
meanwhile I own ancient pain
because I have a myriad of memories of the Sixties
I put my plans on hold and rarely laughed
in the land of loud noises and vacant stares

EPILOGUE

63. - creative process

when I write
I let you peek behind killing's curtain
and for me
each word I write
is a footprint on the long road home
as I search for the beauty of this world
that never ventured into the free-fire zone

INDEX BY FIRST LINE

First Line	*Poem Number*
a flag sits on a shelf	4
a laid-back holiday	44
all triggers aren't found on guns	57
as I write this poem	61
boot camp isn't a philosophy class	19
corpses strewn randomly across the ridgeline	8
dance with your distractions	16
Didn't fell like waking up dead	23
dipped in vinegar	38
for years I've painted the story of the Nam with words	60
fourth of july fireworks come early	13
he sent a dead letter home	58
how will my life's landscape lie	49
I don't know where you are	55
if you don't want to hear about war	35
I guess the dead	54
integration of the races	59
in the binary black and white world of the Nam	26
in the world of the war zone	7
in the world of war	22
in war	31
it makes you feel good	9
I've got those PTSD blues	25

last Tango with the Nam 5
like an Old Testament prophet 37
like tenement cockroaches 34

mortality on steroids 24
my silence screams at me 45
my tears are older than my children 47

no passport required 12
now I gotta move yesterday's grief 15

oh, to slumber 29

partners of water bo dung 56
passing away Nam-style 6
patiently lurking 10

shadow over there 39
snuggling up to violence as a means of fighting violence 21
Stars everywhere 2

the Animals' "Sky Pilot" 52
the circuitous route of the random battle bullet 28
the flag unfurled 40
the half-life of a well-placed AK-47 round 42
the killing bullet 18
the killing country called the Nam 43
the language and the landscape of my poetry 14
there's the *f-word* 20
There were too many dead 30
the script 50
the soul saturated in ancient anguish 32
the teacher's red pen was a deadly dagger 33

tinnitus is no Roman general	46
trolling for a dance partner	51
twenty is the limbo year	41
War and Peace, Hamlet	17
war is a four-letter word	3
war is deceptively simple	1
when I write	63
when the math of mayhem is in session	11
words	48
you babble your euphemisms	62
you cover your pain with a cynical mask	53
you crave gentle words that sing you sleep	36
young love	27

ABOUT THE AUTHOR

Born in New York City, Peter Bourret, a proud grandfather and father of two sons, has lived in Tucson, Arizona for over sixty years; he attended twelve years of Catholic school, graduating from Salpointe Catholic in 1965. He served with the 1st Battalion, 7th Marine Regiment, 1st Marine Division as an 81mm mortarman in Vietnam during 1967 and 1968. He graduated from the University of Arizona in 1971 and received his Masters Degree from the U of A in 1974; he volunteered with a local adult education program for several years and taught social studies for seven years at Apollo Middle School; he also taught English for eighteen years, seventeen of them at Sahuaro High School. Currently retired, he is in the process of writing his memoir, has written a soon-to-be published novel and is preparing a third book of poetry for publication. His interests are eclectic: he dabbles in photography and was a candidate for the school board in Tucson in 1976. An avid hiker, he has traveled extensively, including two return trips to Vietnam in 1991 and 1999. During the Bosnian War in 1993, he brought humanitarian aid to Bosnian refugees. During the early 1980s, he was a crisis counselor with Divorce Recovery of Tucson and was also a co-facilitator of several of their support groups. Recently, he has volunteered in the local public schools, teaching writing to second and tenth graders and has supported a school in Nicaragua with books. He is a charter member of Detachment 1344 of the Marine Corps League and is a life member of Vietnam Veterans of America. Currently, he volunteers at the VA, working with veterans who are experiencing PTSD symptoms; also, he sponsors a monthly coffee and discussion group with World War 2 and Korean War veterans. The subject of *Strands of Barbed Wire*, a documentary about his first return trip to Vietnam, he also has been a guest speaker in high school American History classes on the topic of the Vietnam War experience for the past twenty-five years. He was awarded 1st Place for "Alone with *it* on Veterans Day" in the personal experience category, which he presented at the 2014 National Veterans Creative Arts Festival; additionally, he has won 1st Place for his writing in 2015 and 2017. *War: a memoir*, a narrative about his PTSD interwoven with two dozen of his poems, was published online during the summer of 2014 by The Writers' Circle, Inc. @ www.riwriterscircle.com . *The Physics of War: Poems of War and Healing,* his first book of poetry, was published in January of 2015; *Land of Loud Noises and Vacant Stares,* his second book of poetry, was published in March of 2015 and *Snowflakes from the Other Side of the Universe,* his third book of poetry, was published in August of 2015. *Three Joss Sticks In The Rain,* his first novel, was published in October 2016; and *Jello's Nam: A Memoir* was published in July of 2018. The author is currently finishing his fourth book of poetry and is working on the sequel to his memoir. When Bourret isn't writing, he presents poetry readings and teaches classes about PTSD to varied audiences.

ABOUT THE ARTIST

Artist: Denham Clements

Born: 1944 (Miami Beach, Florida, USA)

Lived/Active: Taos and Albuquerque, New Mexico

Profession: Painter

Known for: Portrait, Western, Botanical, Mixed Media

Style(s): Photo Realist, Contemporary, Mixed Media

Medium(s): Oil, Acrylic, Mixed Media

STUDIED:
Florida State University, BS in Business Administration;
Major: Advertising & Public Relations...1962-66
Self-taught (career began in 1975 in Taos, NM.)
University of New Mexico, 1986...Oil painting, Art
Theory, Modern Art History, Drawing

HONORS:
Who's Who In America, 2013

2014 – The VA's "National Veterans Creative Arts
Festival" Milwaukee, WI   First Place "Military Combat
Experience"; Best of Show

ONGOING EXHIBITIONS:
Albuquerque Museum, part of the permanent collection
"Common Ground", the Museum's Permanent Collection,
Albuquerque, NM
Tucson Museum of Art, part of the permanent collection
"Art of the American West", Tucson, AZ

SOLO EXHIBITIONS:
2003 – Caesarea Gallery, Boca Raton, FL
1998 – Culiver Cadillac & The Book Vine, Scottsdale, AZ
1997 – The Book Vine, Scottsdale, Arizona
1981 – P, M & Stein Gallery, New York, New York
1979 – The Foundry, Washington, DC
1979 – Gallery Allene, Annapolis, Maryland

The origins of the artist's "Vietnam Elegy" began "on the
23rd of November of 2011 after 42 years of sorting through
the personal memories, as well as reflecting on the impact
that a polarized America in the Sixties had on the outcome
of the Vietnam War, I took the road less traveled once
again and began a major mixed media piece that would
become a narrative on canvas that provided a general sense
of the mood and the realities of the Vietnam War era, as
well as take a look at the attitude and events that typified
the happenings back in "the world". As I began my
research it soon became apparent that this was going to be a
complex undertaking and was going to be a lot more than a
guy in a foxhole kind of painting. It is dedicated,
specifically, to all combat Marines of that era, but also
memorializes the veterans of all services, and their families,
who sacrificed so much in the service of a country that was
not all together in support of their mission. "Vietnam
Elegy" was completed on 20 February 2014. Please visit
vietnamelegy.com for an in-depth look at the project, the
process, and its future."

93

Made in the USA
San Bernardino, CA
03 August 2020

76407314R00060